ABOUT THE BANK STREET READY-TO-READ SERIES

More than seventy-five years of educational research, innovative teaching, and quality publishing have earned The Bank Street College of Education its reputation as America's most trusted name in early childhood education.

Because no two children are exactly alike in their development, the Bank Street Ready-to-Read series is written on three levels to accommodate the individual stages of reading readiness of children ages three through eight.

○ *Level 1:* GETTING READY TO READ **(Pre-K–Grade 1)**
Level 1 books are perfect for reading aloud with children who are getting ready to read or just starting to read words or phrases. These books feature large type, repetition, and simple sentences.

● *Level 2:* READING TOGETHER **(Grades 1–3)**
These books have slightly smaller type and longer sentences. They are ideal for children beginning to read by themselves who may need help.

○ *Level 3:* I CAN READ IT MYSELF **(Grades 2–3)**
These stories are just right for children who can read independently. They offer more complex and challenging stories and sentences.

All three levels of The Bank Street Ready-to-Read books make it easy to select the books most appropriate for your child's development and enable him or her to grow with the series step by step. The levels purposely overlap to reinforce skills and further encourage reading.

We feel that making reading fun is the single most important thing anyone can do to help children become good readers. We hope you will become part of Bank Street's long tradition of learning through sharing.

The Bank Street College of Education

For a free color catalog describing Gareth Stevens' list of high-quality books and multimedia programs, call 1-800-542-2595 (USA) or 1-800-461-9120 (Canada). Gareth Stevens Publishing's Fax: (414) 225-0377. See our catalog, too, on the World Wide Web: http://gsinc.com

Library of Congress Cataloging-in-Publication Data

Reit, Seymour.
 The rebus bears / by Seymour Reit; illustrated by Kenneth Smith.
  p. cm. -- (Bank Street ready-to-read)
 Summary: A simple retelling of Goldilocks and the three bears in rebus form.
  ISBN 0-8368-1750-8 (lib. bdg.)
 1. Rebuses. [1. Folklore. 2. Bears--Folklore. 3. Rebuses.]
 I. Smith, Kenneth, ill. II. Goldilocks and the three bears.
 English. III. Title. IV. Series.
 PZ8.3.R28Rj 1997
 398.22
 [E]--DC21   97-1367

This edition first published in 1997 by
Gareth Stevens Publishing
1555 North RiverCenter Drive, Suite 201
Milwaukee, Wisconsin 53212 USA

Bank Street Ready-to-Read™

The Rebus Bears

by Seymour Reit
Illustrated by Kenneth Smith

A Byron Preiss Book

Gareth Stevens Publishing
MILWAUKEE

Once there were **3** brown

bears . . .

a great big Dad bear,

a middle-sized Mom bear,

and a very small young

bear.

The 3 brown bears

lived in a little house

with a purple door.

One day Dad bear made

a big pot

of soup for supper.

The small young bear

set the table with

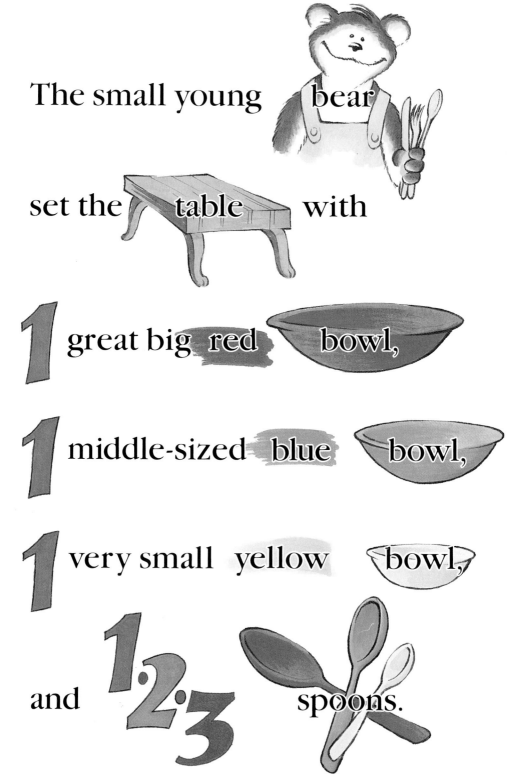

1 great big red bowl,

1 middle-sized blue bowl,

1 very small yellow bowl,

and 123 spoons.

6

Then Mom bear poured

the soup from the pot

into the 3 bowls.

But when the bears

tasted the soup,

that soup from the pot

was too HOT!

Mom  bear said,

"Let's go for a walk.

By the time we get back

to the  house,

the soup will be

So they put on their

 hats,

and they went for a walk
in the woods.

While the **3** bears were away,

a little **girl** named Goldilocks

walked by their house.

The **purple door** was open,

so Goldilocks walked in.

She saw the 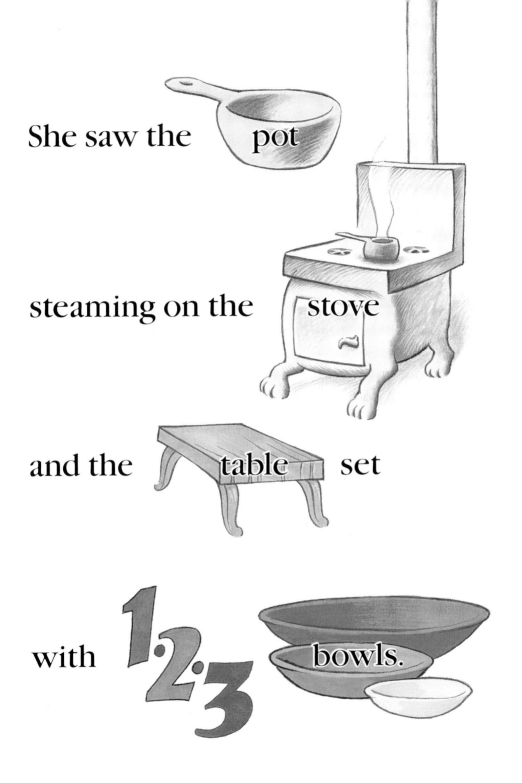 pot

steaming on the stove

and the table set

with 1, 2, 3 bowls.

Her eyes told  Goldilocks

there was something in those

 bowls. Her nose

told her it was something good.

Her mouth said, "Taste it!"

And that's just what she did.

First   Goldilocks   tasted the soup

in the great big red   bowl.

It was too HOT!

Next she tasted the soup in the

middle-sized blue   bowl.

It was too COLD.

Then she tasted the soup in the

very small   yellow  bowl.

That soup was just right.

SIP-SUP!

She ate it all up.

After sipping all that soup,

Goldilocks decided to sit down.

She looked around and saw

chairs.

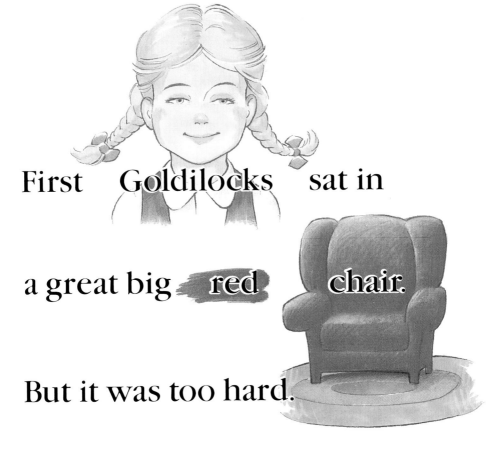

First Goldilocks sat in

a great big red chair.

But it was too hard.

Next she sat in a

middle-sized blue chair.

It was too soft.

Then Goldilocks sat in

a very small yellow  chair.

And it was just right!

She sat down with a plop.

The chair flopped right over!

17

That's when Goldilocks

saw the stairs.

Up, up, up she went.

Upstairs she saw 1, 2, 3

beds.

Seeing the  beds

made Goldilocks sleepy.

She took off her shoes

and lay down on the big
red bed.

It was much too hard.

Next she lay down on

the middle-sized blue   bed.

It was much too soft.

Then she lay down

on the very small   yellow

bed.

And it was just right.

Goldilocks closed her eyes
and fell fast asleep.

After a little while

the  bears

came back.

When they walked through

the   purple   door,

Dad   bear   let out a roar!

"Someone's been sitting

in my red chair!"

Mom bear growled,

"Someone's been sitting

in my blue chair!"

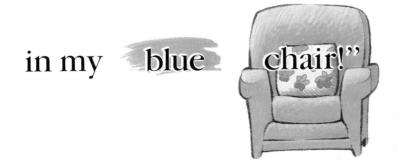

Then the very small young bear

cried, "Someone's been sitting

in my   yellow   chair!

And it flopped over!"

Just then the bears

saw the 3 bowls.

"Someone's been sipping

from my red bowl,"

said Dad bear.

"And someone's been sipping

from my blue bowl,"

said Mom bear.

"Someone's been sipping

from my yellow  bowl,"

said the very small young

 bear.

"And my soup is all gone."

"Let's look upstairs," said Mom

bear.   So, up, up, up

the   stairs   they went.

"Someone's been sleeping in my

bed,"   Dad   bear   said.

"Someone's been sleeping in my

bed," Mom bear said.

The very small young bear said,

"Someone's been sleeping

in my bed.

And there she is!"

Goldilocks opened her eyes

and saw **1, 2, 3** brown

bears

looking down at her.

She jumped up.

She raced down the stairs,

scooted through the

door, and ran home

as fast as her legs could carry her.

And what did the  bears do?

They went down the stairs,

sat on their chairs,

poured soup from the pot,

and it wasn't too HOT!

SIP-SUP! SIP-SUP! SIP-SUP!

They had a fine soup supper.